KU-308-243

These blasphemies, these ecstasies, these cries,
these groans and curses, tears and *Te Deums*,
re-echo through a thousand labyrinths —
a holy opium for mortal hearts!

This, O Lord, is the best evidence
that we can offer of our dignity,
this sob that swells from age to age and dies
out on the shore of Your eternity!

Introduction

Blasphemies, Ecstasies, Cries breaks with the habitual forms of the public presentation of art and by implication the assumptions that lie behind them. It does so by the way the artists have participated, by the way it presents works by living, early 20th, 19th and 17th century artists, by the way it is hung, by the way the information that customarily accompanies works of art is marginalised and by the way it juxtaposes images with text.

Each work in the exhibition is accompanied by lines or stanzas from a poem, *Les Fleurs du Mal*. Each poem has the same two authors: a nineteenth century French poet, Baudelaire, and a twentieth century American translator, Richard Howard. Apart from its vivacity, the translation is chosen because its historical moments and its author are ambiguous. Its language is contemporary, its imagery is nineteenth century. Who is the author, Howard or Baudelaire?

The living artists in the exhibition were asked to choose some lines or verses from the translation to be juxtaposed with one of their pictures. The work could be either an existing one or be made specially for the exhibition. Alternatively, artists could opt to have the curator choose either, or both a work and the lines to accompany it. In the case of the deceased artists, some of the works did have a previous connection with *Les Fleurs du Mal*, others not.

The intention of presenting each work without its maker's name, the date of its creation or any existing title is to undermine and question the customary information by which we are invited to order our experience of art. Central to the modern culture of art is the idea of the artist. The artist's name, always prominently displayed next to the picture in public exhibitions, triggers and channels understanding of a work into the context of a particular reputation, biography and art history.

Picture titles focus attention and suggest connections, pictures are interpreted in their light. Titles can suggest how a work was 'intended' to be interpreted and so we construct an idea of the artist's mind rather than an understanding of the work.

All these cues — names, dates, titles — are tacit invitations to order our understanding in the same ways as museums and retrospective exhibitions are ordered. The argument of this exhibition is not that such devices are without insights and explanatory power, but it proposes to show works in a way that pushes these narratives to the margin. It asks the visitor to experience and make understandings of particular works in other ways.

The paintings, drawings and photographs in the exhibition are not intended to illustrate the text in any literal sense. By bringing together text and image both will be changed and new meanings generated. For instance, a few lines taken from their context may well suggest meanings quite new, quite different from those same lines within the poems. In some cases a brief quotation and image together suggest a synthetic understanding without precedent in the verse or picture. In all cases we re-see poem and picture.

The presence of the text stems from the conviction that there is no such thing as a textless work of art. Conventional art history provides the managerial discourse, the master text, for institutionalised art. Both making and looking at art are informed by a multitude of texts. To look, for example, at a work in terms of pure form is to look at it in the light of a particular tradition of texts on art and aesthetic experience. In particular, the translation serves to usurp the narratives that are implied by name and date. The exhibition replaces the professional prose of art history and criticism with lines from imaginative literature.

There are relatively few works in the exhibition. The number of works and the manner of hanging are intended to suggest to the visitor prolonged attention to individual pictures. To escape the anaemic blandness of the 'white gallery', each picture is given its own space, emphasised by differently coloured backgrounds. Strategies to homogenise the hanging have been abandoned towards a positively 'inconsistent', individual approach.

Blasphemies, Ecstacies, Cries is an exhibition that denies essences. It denies there is an essential *Les Fleurs du Mal*, there are only readings of it of which this translation is one. It denies that there is some essence signalled by the name of an artist by which we must formulate our understandings of his or her work. It denies that a title or a date provides information essential for an understanding of a work of art.

These departures aim to place art in the context of imaginative culture rather than explanatory discourses. *Blasphemies, Ecstasies, Cries* invites the visitor to make sense of each particular juxtaposition of image and words. Both are imaginative statements. They call for reflective understanding rather than art historical management.

Acknowledgements

On behalf of the Serpentine Gallery I would like to thank the guest-curator for his proposal to make this exhibition, and all the dedicated work that followed, as well as for his substantial contribution to the catalogue.

Together, we are grateful to John Goto for producing the textpanels for the exhibition. Above all, thanks are due to the artists and lenders for their courage and enthusiasm to participate in a project that deviates so uncompromisingly from conventional exhibition practices.

BLASPHEMIES, ECSTASIES, CRIES

Baudelaire as Anti-Modernist

Art looks for its resources of conviction in the same general direction as thought. Once it was revealed religion, then it was hypostatizing reason. The nineteenth century shifted its quest to the empirical and positive. The notion of the empirical and the positive has undergone much revision over the last hundred years, and generally become stricter and perhaps narrower. Aesthetic sensibility has shifted accordingly. The growing specialization of the arts is due chiefly not to the prevalence of the division of labour, but to an increasing faith in and taste for the immediate, the concrete, the irreducible. To meet this taste, the various modernist arts try to confine themselves to the most positive and immediate in themselves.
Clement Greenberg, *Art and Culture*, 1961

This essay uses Baudelaire as a critic of the Modernism Greenberg describes. But Modernism is taken to be primarily an institutionalised way of understanding art rather than a kind of art. It sketches a socio-historical story in which Modernism is shown as rooted in the logic of modern management; Modernism as one of the discourses of control. The essay describes what *Blasphemies, Ecstasies, Cries* breaks with and why the exhibition and catalogue explore images as companions and translations of another kind of discourse.

By discourses is meant ways of ordering things, ways of understanding. The medium of human consciousness is language. The language we enter when we achieve consciousness has been created in social life, which is to say, in particular forms of social life. Particular forms of life and areas of activity generate and order the world through particular language uses or discourses. What is assumed in the essay is that how we experience and act in the world depends on the discourses in which we have our consciousness.

I. From Fable and Legend to Modern History

In the hanging of the Louvre between the late 1960s and 1987 the Salle Mollien, the Pavilion Denon and Salle Daru presented a chronological story of French late eighteenth and nineteenth century painting.

The walls were dominated by huge canvasses. They offered dramatic spaces animated by gesturing figures: physiognomy, the disposition of draper, glance, musculature and stance expressed human passions and created gravity-defying rhythms. These were and are History Paintings. Their themes came from classical history and myth, from the Bible and literature.

Hanging at the end of the Salle Daru was a painting made in a time of leftist militancy in France. It is of equal or greater scale to many of those that preceded it. *History Painting of a Burial at Ornans*, to give it its full title, depicts a small town funeral. Rather than defying gravity its rhythms repeat the literal horizontal of the ground. Movement is muffled by its shallow space and the undifferentiated coagulation of figures in black. Mundane inexpressive faces are caricatured in thick, opaque and encrusted paint. Christian ceremony is mocked as jejeune. But it too is a History Painting.

This pictorial rhetoric claims factuality. Its literature, the discursive world the painting presupposed, was current political and social theory. In such theory the facts of social life had become the object of examination; they now constituted history.

The position of this picture and the preceding works implied a story of art's development in France in the nineteenth century; the advance of art from Classicism through Romanticism to Realism, a heroic tale of great artists at odds with "bourgeois" taste. It was a story supposedly consummated in the eventual triumph of Modernism.

Courbet's *History Painting of a Burial at Ornans* did foreshadow Modernism in that it was an assault upon imaginative culture. It divorced painting from literature and placed it in social and political discourse. It is a Positivist painting. The Burial was made in the light of "scientific" social theory.

By Positivism is meant the belief that scientific rationality is the paradigm for all knowledge. The term was coined by Auguste Comte who envisaged the whole of human culture ordered by scientific method. Amongst the positive sciences was social physics, Comte re-named it sociology. In Comte's conception future society should be led by sociologists.

In a book written in ten or so years after the *Burial* was painted, the socialist theorist Pierre-Joseph Proudhon wrote that Courbet was an expression of his time and his work coincided with Proudhon's own and Comte's.

Before Courbet emerged on the public arena, Proudhon has, like others, looked forward to a new positive art: 'We can hope one day to attain a theory of beauty in which painting, architecture and sculpture will be treated like exact sciences, such that artistic composition will be similar to the construction of a ship, the integration of a mathematical curve, or the calculation of stress and strain . . . the rational production of beauty will outreach the marvels of spontaneous inspiration, just as modern science surpasses ancient fables and the philosophy of history surpasses legend'.

What 'the philosophy of history' meant was the modern idea of progress; the idea that humankind advances through instrumental knowledge. By disposing of legend and fable humankind could rationally shape its future. Now systematic knowledge of the past and the present societies would provide instrumental social knowledge, just as physics was thought to have laid the basis for modern technology.

Burial at Ornans is an image of social knowledge. Its politics, how it related to power, should be understood in the light of the politics of knowledge.

II. The Social Basis of the Avant Garde

Opposite the *Burial* in both its former position in the Louvre and in its new location in the Musée d'Orsay is another huge picture. In its centre is an artist painting. A grouping of figures occupies the left of the canvas and another group occupies the right. In *The painter's studio: A real allegory summing up seven years of my artistic life,* Courbet paints himself at the centre and arrays all else around him.

'It is society at the top, bottom and middle. In a word, it is my way of seeing society in its interests and passions. It is the world come to be painted at my place. . .', wrote Courbet of the painting. He went on: 'The scene takes place in my atelier in Paris. The painting is divided into two parts. I am in the middle painting. To the right are the shareholders [les actionnaires], that is to say, [my] friends, [my fellow] workers, and amateurs from the art world. To the left is the other world of the trivial life, the people, misery, poverty, wealth, the exploited, people who live on death . . .'

The social division Courbet set up was not a confrontation of bourgeoisie and proletariat; the 'exploited' and 'exploiters' occupy only the left of the canvas. The division was between those that support his art and the rest. But this autobiographical choice of friends and colleagues (including Proudhon) from advanced political and artistic circles were from a particular social group; most of them were professional intellectuals.

Courbet painted his effectual audience, the avant-garde audience that shared his cultural matrix. It is an image of a new bourgeoisie. While it included two rich collectors — art lovers, 'amateurs', it consisted predominantly of people who, like himself, were changing from one kind of bourgeois into another. While their parents owned financial capital, these men were developing careers in which they derived their status, power and, some, their incomes from cultural capital, from knowledge. This bourgeoisie was the social basis of avant-garde art and politics.

Their commitment to the removal of power from the monied bourgeoisie and creation of a society ordered by rational knowledge should be seen in this light. In other words, their socialism and positivism is ideological in the simple sense of expressing a class interest. Courbet's work and the image of his 'fellow workers' is a glimpse of the nascent New Class.

It was in an attack upon Marx that Bakunin predicted that a society in which there was government but no privileged class would give rise to 'the reign of scientific intelligence . . .

There will be a new class, a new hierarchy of real and pretended scientists and scholars'. The idea of the New Class now has a large literature.

In this essay the New Class is seen as arising with modern means of production, distribution and communication. In the period since the industrial revolution, traditional intellectual professions have been transformed and new bodies of expertise peculiar to modern society have come into existence. The New Class has power through both the private and public sectors: it stretches from academics to accountants, from scientists to civil servants, from media people to judges.

The New Class has come to share and in some instances wrestle power from the old bourgeoisie. While defined by its ownership of highly valued cultural capital, it is a complex and heterogenous class. Many of the critics of its ideology have come from within itself.

At either edge of the *Studio* are emblems of financial and cultural capital. On the far left, in the world of exploiters and exploited, stands a man holding a money box. The figure on the extreme right, in the world of Courbet's fellow workers, holds a book.

III. Baudelaire's Anti-Positivism

The figure at the very right hand edge of the *Studio* holding a book is an image of Charles Baudelaire.

The *Studio* was exhibited on the fringe of the Exposition Universelle of 1855. Baudelaire reviewed the Exposition and briefly discussed Courbet: he likened him to Ingres in his 'immolation' of imagination, 'but the difference is that the heroic sacrifice offered by M. Ingres in honour of the idea and the tradition of Raphaelesque Beauty is performed by M. Courbet on behalf of external, positive and immediate Nature'.

While there is only brief mention of Courbet, much of the review can be read as anti-realist, anti-positivist and anti-progressive tract; as an attack, in other words, upon the artistic doctrines of which Courbet was the most notorious pictorial practitioner.

Positivism holds there is no metaphysical order behind appearance. Baudelaire opens his review by asserting a universal analogy in which plants and nations are 'more or less spiritual'. There is the order of things known only to 'him who is indefinable'. Whereas Positivism has at its centre the belief that the world can be known, Baudelaire here insists on the un-knowable.

Positivism looks forward to a unified scientific method that would legislate for all areas of activity, as exampled by Proudhon's prediction of an exact science of beauty. 'Beauty is always strange', asserts Baudelaire. He has abandoned systematic criticism, denounces 'modern aesthetic pundits' and claims as a critic to speak only 'in the name of feeling, of morality and of pleasure'.

Rather than write on pictorial technicalities, 'you will find me appraising a picture exclusively for the sum of ideas or of dreams that it suggests to my mind'. In other words, each work is to give rise to its own specific understanding rather than being subjected to a general professional discourse.

Positivism understands history as progress through the growth of knowledge. Baudelaire condemns the idea of progress: 'this modern lantern throws a stream of darkness upon all objects of knowledge'. Because we have lost the capacity to distinguish between the 'physical and the moral world' we believe by technological progress we have surpassed the ancients.

Baudelaire castigates the application of the idea of progress to the sphere of the imagination as a 'gigantic absurdity'. He dismisses art as an evolution in which each artist is begat by his predecessors: 'The artist stems only from himself'. This points the specificity of an artist's work rather than making it the subject of a historical narrative. Again Baudelaire can be understood as attacking the ideas that order what has become the professional presentation and understanding of art.

The last part of the review praises Delacroix for antithetical characteristics to those he attributed to Courbet: whereas Courbet was concerned with the external, Delacroix reveals what lies behind nature; Courbet presents the positive, Delacroix conveys the vague and sinuous; Courbet waged war upon imagination, for Baudelaire, Delacroix was the modern exemplar of the imaginative artist.

Courbet's painting constituted a rejection of imaginative literature. Baudelaire in praising Delacroix uses what has become a term of disapprobation in Modernist criticism; Delacroix's talent, he says, is essentially 'literary'. Baudelaire goes on to push the term beyond allusion to literature, 'not only has his art ranged over the field of the great literatures of the world; not only has it translated, and been the companion of, Ariosto, Byron, Dante, Scott and Shakespeare, but it has the power of revealing ideas of a loftier, a subtler and a deeper order than the arts of the majority of modern painters'.

IV. The Invisible Text

'Courbet himself belongs to the period of transition from the cultivated artist of historical painting, who moves with an elaborate baggage of literature, history and philosophy and whose works have to be understood as well as seen, to the artist of the second half of the nineteenth century, who relies on sensibility alone, working directly from nature or from feeling, an eye rather than a mind or an imagination. Besides the great masters of the preceding period, this newer type of artist was for a critic like Baudelaire a mere artisan, ignorant and plebeian'.

This was written in 1941 by one of the most brilliant of modern art historians, Meyer

Schapiro. But what he states is misleading if it is taken as ignoring the plurality of art in modern times. There is hardly any kind of art made in Courbet's time or subsequently that did not continue to be practised and that is not now being practised.

Furthermore, to give just four instances to stand for a legion, Gustave Moreau, Edward Burne-Jones, Lovis Corinth, Mikhail Vrubel were all painters of the latter half of the nineteenth century and overtly alluded to literature in their work.

Imaginative literature, philosophy and history have rarely ceased to be part of the culture that prompted avant-garde and other forms of serious modern art. But its role has been marginalised. The literature of modernist art is the professional discourse of the institutions of modern art. Clement Greenberg spells out as principle what is implicit in the logic of modern institutionalised art when he uses 'literary' to describe meanings forced into pictorial art which do not, in his view, properly belong to it.

Professional discourse is the invisible text that lies behind the near textless display of art in museums and art galleries. The names of artists, the date of a work and its title are the visible tips of icebergs of narratives and information that select, order and display art.

V. MOMA and the Ordering of Modern Art

Museums remove things from particular forms of life. For much modern art the museum has become the centre of its form of life, the institutional centre of its discourse. The pioneer of the institutionalisation of modern art is the Museum of Modern Art, New York. Its ideology has been a source and its collection a paradigm for the new profession that has emerged with the post-war boom in modern art institutions.

'This institution', wrote William Rubin, the current Director of MOMA's Department of Painting and Sculpture, 'saw modern art as an international movement, none of whose parts could be eliminated without deforming the image of its development'.

This "international" view, this invisible text, perceives Paris as the centre of modern art until 1940 and then New York — central Europe, the USSR, South America are peripheral and Asia, Africa and Western popular and traditionalist art are hardly seen.

These exclusions and hierarchies *hide things* from sight, but the effect of the developmental narrative is also on *how things* are seen. MOMA's pictures are hung so their internal life does not disrupt the general story of modern art as told by the museum's display: white walls, pictures uniformly framed in narrow dark brown or black battens, the visual effect is to assert the picture as a hued surface and to bleach out its tonal life and fictive depth.

Much of the contemporary art given institutional recognition since the late 1950s has been art in a minor genre created by MOMA more than any other institution, the genre of art for museums.

VI. The New Class and the Discourses of Control

The professionalisation of art in the post-1945 period was part of the much wider rise of the New Class in both the public and private sectors. For example, the growth of the civil service and financial institutions gave political and economic power to people ostensibly qualified for their positions by professional expertise.

The New Class are the masters of the diverse discourses of control. But, as Alvin Gouldner argued in his book *The Future of Intellectuals and the Rise of the New Class*, they share within and across disciplines common rules of speech, they share what he calls the culture of critical discourse.

'The culture of critical discourse is characterised by speech that is *relatively* more *situation-free*, more context or field "independent." This speech culture thus values expressly legislated meanings and devalues tacit, context-limited meanings. Its ideal is: "one word, one meaning," for everyone and forever.'

The positivism of this speech culture lies primarily in its aspiration to be systematic, progressive and universal. Comte dreamt of sociology as the master discourse but in the West the discourses of control are divided into professional cultures. The term Modernism has been used in this essay to mean primarily the professional discourse that orders and institutionalises art within the ideology of the New Class.

The poverty of imagination and fictive space in so much of the officially acknowledged art of our time stems from the redundance of imagery in work given meaning by the modern institutionalised culture of art. In the opening quotation of this essay Greenberg both offers an explanation for and celebrates this imaginative poverty, but the taste for 'the immediate, the concrete and the irreducible' has not been a general taste, it is a professional initiate taste.

The cultural events heralded as the decline of Modernism are in part the victory of a more rigorous professional discourse rather than its end. The heroic story of avant-garde art and artists stands exposed as legend and fable by an art history increasingly absorbed into social history.

Now that Courbet's *Burial* and the *Studio* hang in the Musée d'Orsay, he is no longer the single heroic realist but one of many on display. Thomas Couture was an 'eclectic' rival and contemporary of Courbet. Raised from the obscurity to which the old story had consigned it as aesthetically reactionary, his huge *Romans in the Period of Decadence* faces Courbet's work across the great hall of the d'Orsay. The plurality of modern art is now admitted.

In *Blasphemies, Ecstasies, Cries* Modernism is not assumed to be prompting and encompassing discourse of all avant-garde and serious modern art. Once Modernism's invisible text is made visible and the idea that art 'speaks for itself' is dismissed, then the question is no longer text or no text, but which and what kind of texts. This exhibition and its catalogue breaks with the orthodox discourse to explore just one avenue. That it is an avenue sympathetic to what prompts some very able artists is indicated by their willingness to participate in the exhibition and by the fact that it was not difficult to find pictures that gained a different vivacity by juxtaposition with the poetry of Baudelaire/Howard.

It is a profoundly reactionary exhibition in that it sets out to recoup imaginative high culture rather than revolutionise it.

VII. Imaginative High Culture

Blasphemies, Ecstasies, Cries advocates and examples the location of serious image-making in European imaginative high culture rather than in the professional discourse of art.

By European imaginative high culture is meant a culture of images and utterances that speaks of the world through fictions, that offers understanding rather than instrumental knowledge. By high it is meant that it is a reflective and self-aware culture and that it makes demands peculiar to itself by its alienation from banal culture.

The novel is a paradigm of the discourse of modern imaginative high culture. Milan Kundera, in his essay, "The Novel and Europe" wrote: 'The novel's essence is complexity. Every novel says to the reader: "Things are not as simple as you think." That is the novel's eternal truth, but its voice grows ever fainter in a world based upon easy quick answers that come before and rule out the question. In this world, it's either Anna or Karenin who is right, and the ancient wisdom of Cervantes, which speaks of the difficulty of knowing and of a truth that eludes the grasp, seems cumbersome and useless."

He goes on to say at the end of his essay: "But if the idea of progress arouses my suspicion, what are the values to which I feel attached? God? Fatherland? People? The Individual?

My answer is as sincere as it is ridiculous: I am attached to nothing apart from the European novel, that unrecognised inheritance that comes to us from Cervantes.'

As Kundera implies for the novel, imaginative high culture makes no claims to universality, it is informed primarily by the European tradition of literature and art. Nor is it progressive, we have not refuted Cervantes or the ancients, nor is it systematic, it speaks through the polyvalence of words and images.

The title of Charles Baudelaire's poem 'Les Phares' is usually translated as 'Beacons
. The poem in a series of four-line stanzas celebrate the work of Rubens, Leanardo, Rembrandt, Michelangelo, Watteau, Puget, Goya and Delacroix. In Richard Howard's translation of *Les Fleurs du Mal* he entitles it 'Guiding Lights'. Two of the closing verses read:

These blasphemies, these ecstasies, these cries,
these groans and curses, tears and *Te Deums*,
re-echo through a thousand labyrinths —
a holy opium for mortal hearts!

This, O Lord, is the best evidence
that we can offer of our dignity,
this sob that swells from age to age and dies
out on the shore of Your eternity!

To echo Kundera, I can think of no more commanding adherence than these blasphemies,
these ecstasies, these cries.

And all beguile me, but especially
those who, honeying their pain, implore
Addiction that had once lent them its wings:
'Mighty Hippogriff, let my fly again!'

and every colour, even black,
    became a lustrous prism;
liquid turned to glowing glass
    and what was crystal flowed;

Daughter of darkness, slattern deity
rank with musk and nicotine, the spawn
of filthy covens or a shaman's rites
ebony fetish, nameless talisman . . . And yet

to wine, to opium even, I prefer
the elixir of your lips on which love flaunts
itself; and in the wasteland of desire
your eyes afford the wells to slake my thirst.

Seal them, those sooty holes from which your soul
rains hellfire too, relentless sorceress!
I am no Styx, to cradle you nine times,

alas! and cannot with some Fury's lust,
to break your spirit and your heart, become
in your bed's inferno . . . Persephone!

BLASPHEMIES, ECSTASIES, CRIES

pillow of flesh where no dream is of love
but where life seethes and surges endlessly
like wind in heaven, sea within a sea

As you dance by, beloved indolence
— the music fading, though it fills the room —
you seem to hover in your listlessness,
and boredom glistens in your heavy glance;

No rage, no rancour: I shall beat you
    as butchers fell an ox,
as Moses smote the rock in Horeb —
    I shall make you weep,

and by the waters of affliction
    my desert will be slaked.
My desire, that hope has made monstrous
    will frolic in your tears

as a ship tosses on the ocean —
    in my besotted heart
your adorable sobs will echo
    like an ecstatic drum.

For I — am I not a dissonance
    in the divine accord,
because of the greedy Irony
    which infiltrates my soul?

I hear it in my voice — that shrillness,
    that poison in my blood!
I am the sinister glass in which
    the Fury sees herself!

I am the knife and the wound it deals,
    I am the slap and the cheek,
I am the wheel and the broken limbs,
    hangman and victim both!

I am the vampire at my own veins,
    one of the great lost horde
doomed for the rest of time, and beyond,
    'to laugh — but smile no more.'

O draw the curtains — leave the world outside!
There must be rest for all this weariness.
Let me annihilate myself upon
your breast and find the solace of the grave!'

To fallen man, who suffers and dreams on,
the Empyrean's inaccessible blue
presents the fascination of the Void.

pursue what Plato's scowling eyes condemn

and win your pardon for the martyrdom
forever inflicted on ambitious hearts . . .

What use to us are laws of right and wrong?
High-hearted virgins, honour of Isles,
your altars are august as any: love
will laugh at Heaven as it laughs at Hell!
What use to us are laws of right and wrong?

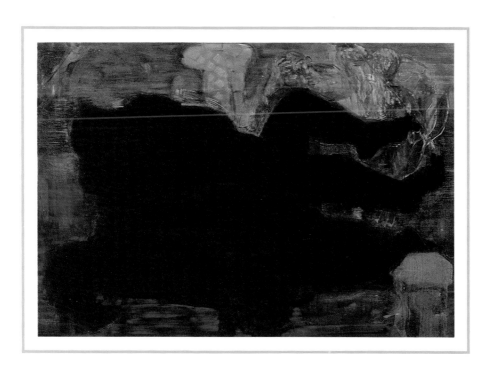

Each of you in his heart has worshipped me,
in secret kissed my filthy ass — behold!
Hear my laugh and welcome Satan home,
    huge and ugly as the earth itself!

Like long-held echoes, blending somewhere else
into one deep and shadowy unison
as limitless as darkness and as day

From their posture, the wise
learn to shun, in this world at least,
        motion and commotion;

impassioned by passing shadows,
        man will always be scourged
for trying to change his place.

Swarming city — city gorged with dreams,
where ghosts by day accost the passer-by

Nature glows with this man's joy,
    dims with another's grief;
what signifies the grave to one
    is glory to the next.

The pillars of Nature's temple are alive
and sometimes yield perplexing messages;
forests of symbols between us and the shrine
remark our passage with accustomed eyes.

Like long-held echoes, blending somewhere else
into one deep and shadowy unison
as limitless as darkness and as day,
the sounds, the scents, the colours correspond.

or an armoire in some abandoned house
acrid with the dust of time itself

Hate is a drunk at the dark end of the bar
whose liquor only makes him thirstier —
a Hydra multiplies at every drop

The coffins of old women are often the size
of a child's, have you ever noticed? Erudite
Death, by making the caskets match, suggests
a tidy symbol, if in dubious taste

When the intolerable weight of your tormented flesh
hung from your distended arms; when blood
and sweat cascaded from your whitening brow;
when you were made target for all eyes —

Ecstatic fleece that ripples to your nape
and reeks of negligence in every curl!

Insolent Eros,
     seated on the skull
     of Humanity
     as if on a throne,
gaily blows bubbles

— She weeps, you fool, for having lived! and for
living — yet what she laments the most,
what makes her body tremble head to toe,
is that tomorrow she will have to live,
and all tomorrows after — like ourselves!

None of the famous landscapes that we saw
equalled the mysterious allure
of those that Chance arranges in the clouds . . .

Race of Abel, your corpse
will fatten the reeking earth;

your labour, Race of Cain,
is not yet done.

I conjured up her natural majesty,
the energy and grace that arm her glance,
the perfumed helmet that her hair creates,
whose memory wakens me to love once more . . .

Wriggling in our brains like a million worms
a demon demos holds its revels there

you whom my soul has followed to your hell,
Sisters! I love you as I pity you
for your bleak sorrows, for your unslaked thirsts,
and for the love that gorges your great hearts!

Illustrations

Gustave Courbet
*History Painting of a Burial
at Ornans* 1849-50
Oil on canvas
312.4 x 663 cm
Musee d'Orsay
(Page 6 top)

Gustave Courbet
*The Artist's Studio: A real
allegory summing up seven
years of
my artistic life* 1855
360 x 597 cm
Musee d'Orsay
(Page 6 bottom)

Avis Newman
Nests there are . . . 1986-87
Mixed media, drawing on
muslin in painted box with
birdswing and honeycomb
38 x 33cm
The Artist, Courtesy Lisson
Gallery
(Page 17)

Frank Auerbach
J. Y. M. Seated in the Studio
1987/88
Oil on canvas
71.8 x 81.9cm
Private Collection
(Page 19)

Gillian Ayres
Song of Poliphile 1987
Oil on canvas
243 x 214.6 cm
Knoedler Kasmin Ltd
(Page 21)

I.H.J.T. Fantin-Latour
Homage to Rubens c. 1880
Oil on canvas
45.7 x 55.8 cm
Southampton City Art
Gallery
(Page 23)

Therese Oulton
Song of Deceit 1988
Oil on canvas
167.6 x 147 cm
Private Collection, Milan
(Page 25)

John Murphy
*I have carved you in the palm
of my hand* 1985
Oil on linen
198.1 x 167.6 cm
Saatchi Collection, London
(Page 27)

Carel Weight
The Friends 1968
Oil on canvas
152.5 x 71cm
The Trustees of the Tate
Gallery
(Page 29)

Arturo Di Stefano
Carphology: Danae 1988
Oil on linen
208.2 x 152.4 cm
The Artist, Courtesy
Pomeroy Purdy Gallery
(Page 31)

Joan Key
*Two Martyrs: After Two
Baroque Sculptures* 1987
Oil on canvas
243 x 167.6 cm
(Page 33)

Auguste Rodin
Satan and his worshipper
c. 1883
Pen, pencil, ink, brown ink
wash and white gouache on
ruled paper
14.6 x 17.8cm
Private Collection
(Page 35)

Richard Hamilton
Lobby 1985-87
Oil on canvas
175 x 250cm
(Page 37)

Craigie Horsfield
*Magda Mierwa ul. Nawojki,
Kraków* August 1984
Photograph
140 x 140cm
(Page 39)

Peter Greenham
This sinister Ancient . . .
1988
Oil on canvas
61 x 50.8 cm
(Page 41)

Andrew Mansfield
Mount Wilson 1986
Oil on canvas
167.6 x 137 cm
The Artist, Courtesy
Anthony Reynolds Gallery
(Page 43)

Stephen McKenna
Pulcinello 1897
Oil on canvas
180 x 120cm
Courtesy Edward Totah
Gallery
(Page 45)

Edmund Fairfax-Lucy
Or some old armoire . . .
1988
Oil on board
45.7 x 55.9cm
(Page 47)

Wyndham Lewis
Self Portrait 1911
Pencil and watercolour
30.5 x 24.1 cm
Collection C. J. Fox
(Page 49)

Francis Bacon
Study of a Child 1960
Oil on canvas
152.5 x 118cm
James Kirkman Ltd, London
(Page 51)

John Goto and Paul Eachus
Field of Entrapment 1986
Oil paint and photographs on
canvas
231 x 218 cm
(Page 53)

Abraham Begeijn
c. 1637-97
Plant Study with Goat
Oil on canvas
35.5 x 31.1cm
Norfolk Museum Service
(Norwich Castle Museum)
(Page 55)

Adam Lowe
Summer 1987
Oil on canvas
247 x 200cm
Collection Michael and
Helen Mallinson
(Page 57)

Frederick Sandys
Mary Magdalen 1862
Oil on canvas
29.2 x 24.8cm
(Page 59)

David Hiscock
The Elysian Fields 1988
Photograph with graphite
and chalk
109 x 99cm
(Page 61)

George Frederick Watts
1817-1904
The Curse of Cain
Oil on canvas
66.1 x 34.2cm
(Page 63)
Norfolk Museum Services
(Norwich Castle Museum)

Jacob Epstein
*Sketch for Baudelaire's
"Fleurs du Mal"* c. 1939
Pencil
23.7 x 37cm
Southampton City Art
Gallery
(Page 65)

Peter de Francia
Wriggling in our brains . . .
1988
Charcoal on paper
55.6 x
(Page 67)

R. B. Kitaj
After Baudelaire 1988
Charcoal and pastel on paper
147 x 58 cm
Marlborough Fine Art
(Page 69)

BLASPHEMIES, ECSTASIES, CRIES

Serpentine Gallery 18 January to 26 February 1989

Exhibition curated by Andrew Brighton
Organised by Andrea Schlieker

Essay by Andrew Brighton
Introduction by Andrew Brighton and Andrea Schlieker

© Serpentine Gallery, Andrew Brighton, the artists 1988

Catalogue designed by Arefin & Arefin
Typeset by Spencers, London
Printed by EGA partnership, Brighton

Published by the Serpentine Gallery in an edition of 1000
ISBN 1 870814 25 8

The quotations on page 2, 3 and 16 to 69 are taken from:
Charles Baudelaire, Les Fleurs du Mal, translated by
Richard Howard, Picador Classics 1987

The exhibition will tour to the
Norwich School of Art Gallery: 17 April to 13 May 1989
Mostyn Gallery, Llandudno: 10 June to 8 July 1989

As an independent educational charity, the Serpentine Gallery
receives financial support from the Arts Council of Great
Britain, and Westminster City Council. To ensure the gallery is
operational throughout the year, further income needs to be
generated from donations, covenants and sponsorship.

Serpentine Gallery, Kensington Gardens, London W2 3XA